D1197906

The Family That Grew

THE FAMILY THAT GREW

By Florence Rondell and Ruth Michaels

Revised Edition Illustrated by Judith Epstein & Tom O'Sullivan

CROWN PUBLISHERS, INC. · NEW YORK

Library of Congress Catalog Card Number: 51-12008

ISBN: 0-517-50107-4

FIRST EDITION—16 PRINTINGS

REVISED EDITION

Ninth Printing, August, 1972

Printed in the United States of America

What's the smallest thing you ever saw?

A pebble?

A raindrop?

A grain of sand?

Once you were even smaller than any of these things. That was before you were born.

Everything living has to start growing. A rooster and a hen start every little chick. A gander and a goose start every little gosling. And a man and a lady start every little baby.

And that's how you started, too.

Like everything starting to grow, you were much too tiny to do a single thing for yourself. So the lady kept you warm, and protected you inside of her body, until you were big enough to eat, and breathe, and cry, and smile.

Then you were big enough to be born, and you were.

Everybody wants to take care of the babies they grow.

Cats want to take care of their kittens.

Dogs want to take care of their puppies.

Ducks want to take care of their ducklings.

When you were born, the lady and the man who started you also wanted to take care of you.

Sometimes, though, something happens so that people cannot take care of the babies they start, and that happened to the lady and the man who started you. So they thought and thought about what they could do to be sure you had a Father and a Mother, to love you and take care of you.

They went to a special person whose job it is to know about children, and the things they need to be happy. They asked her to find the right Father and Mother for you to grow up with, because they wanted you to grow up in a family.

And she found your Mommy and Daddy, who had always wanted a child to cuddle and love. As much as they wanted it, no baby grew inside your Mommy.

When they heard about you, oh, how they wanted to be your Daddy and Mommy, and to have you for their child! Daddy had wanted Mommy for his wife. Mommy had wanted Daddy for her husband. Now both of them wanted you for their child.

This is called adopting a child.

Mommy turned to Daddy, and Daddy turned to Mommy, and both of them said together, "This is the child for us!"

Then they both laughed, because they both wanted you so much. And even though you were a little baby still, and couldn't say a word, you too probably knew how much they wanted you.

Your new Mommy and Daddy were so happy! They bought a new highchair for you to sit in. They bought a new playpen for you

to play in. And they got a new carriage, to wheel you down the street in.

And then they went to the grocery store for the food you would need to make you grow strong. They told the grocer to wrap up his very finest baby-foods, for the wonderful new baby they were adopting as their own.

They carried home bottles to feed you your milk, powder to dust you with, and a beautiful rattle for you to bang.

Then came the best of all — THEY BROUGHT YOU HOME!

Mommy cuddled you in her arms all the way. Daddy grinned every time he looked at you. When you got home, Mommy held you close and fed you. Together, Mommy and Daddy tucked you into your crib. They were so glad you were their baby! And you fell fast asleep, because it was good to be in your new home, with your new parents.

When you woke up, you felt very rested, and that was good, because your whole family was coming to see you.

Your Grandma looked at you, and said, "What a LOVELY baby!"

Your Grandpa looked at you, and said, "What a REMARKABLE baby!" *your Brother Looked At you And SAID "*

All your aunts and uncles and cousins *what a cool dude* looked at you, and said, "What a MAGNIFICENT baby!"

And everybody gave you an extra big hug, because they were so specially glad you were part of their family now.

It was such fun to watch you grow!

One morning, you had a brand new tooth!

Your hair grew so long you needed a very soft brush and a very small comb to keep it out of your eyes.

One fine day, you could sit up in your highchair!

And one exciting afternoon, Mommy called Daddy at work to tell him VERY important news. You had said "Mommy!" and "Daddy!" for the very first time!

First thing you knew, you could walk by yourself. AND YOU WALKED ON YOUR TIPTOES.

Next thing you knew, you could splash in your tub.

Then you could say "More!" when your plate was empty.

By and by, you could even eat by yourself.

And after a while, you could ride your bike, and write with crayons, and build with blocks, and look at picture books, and listen to records.

It was fun to watch you grow bigger and bigger, doing all the things you could not do when you were a baby.

Every day, you and your Mommy and Daddy did things together.

After your Mommy finished the shopping, she took you to the playground, to climb and swing with the other children.

When your Daddy came home from work, he helped you build tall buildings with your blocks.

You and your Mommy and Daddy went to the zoo, and you jabbered at the monkeys. You went on picnics, and rolled in the grass. Sometimes you went visiting, and sometimes company came to see you.

Some days weren't exactly fun, either. Mommy was angry when you ran across the street, without even looking, when you were supposed to wait at the corner for her. Once you were sick, and your throat hurt, and Mommy was sorry. There was the day Mommy was tired and cranky, and you didn't like her so much. AND the night Daddy was bossy, and you didn't like him one bit!

Sometimes you were mad at them, the way every child gets mad at his parents. But even when you were angry at each other, Daddy and Mommy agreed that they loved you, and that it was good to have you for their child.

Every year, of course, you had a birthday and a birthday party—sometimes with Daddy and Mommy, sometimes with other people in your family, sometimes with your friends.

It was always a specially happy day, because you were another year older.

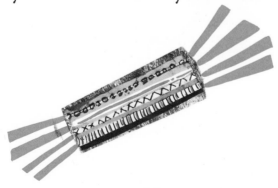

Every birthday, Daddy and Mommy thought again how glad they were that you were born, and that they adopted you. They thought of the many wonderful things you had done together since you were their child, and they were your Father and Mother.

They thought about how they loved you, and took care of you, and watched you grow, and how you played together, and enjoyed one another.

AND THEY ARE GLAD, AND ALWAYS WILL BE, TO HAVE A FAMILY, TO HAVE YOU.